STANDAR for Solo Singers

*12 Contemporary Settings of Favorites
from the Great American Songbook for Solo Voice and Piano*

arranged by **Jay Althouse**

CONTENTS

CD Track Number/Title   **Page**

1. **Anything Goes**
   Cole Porter. 2

2. **At Last**
   Mack Gordon and Harry Warren 9

3. **Blues in the Night**
   Johnny Mercer and Harold Arlen. 12

4. **Don't Get Around Much Anymore**
   Duke Ellington and Bob Russell. 18

5. **Ev'ry Time We Say Goodbye**
   Cole Porter. 22

6. **I Only Have Eyes for You/The More I See You**
   Al Dubin, Mack Gordon, and Harry Warren. 25

7. **Lullaby of Broadway (and Forty-Second Street)**
   Al Dubin and Harry Warren 30

8. **More Than You Know**
   William Rose, Edward Eliscu, and Vincent Youmans 36

9. **Send in the Clowns**
   Stephen Sondheim. 40

10. **Skylark**
    Johnny Mercer and Hoagy Carmichael. 46

11. **Someone to Watch Over Me**
    George Gershwin and Ira Gershwin. 50

12. **Together Wherever We Go**
    Stephen Sondheim and Jule Styne. 55

Background and Historical Information 62

Medium Low Book (27462)   ISBN-10: 0-7390-4713-2   ISBN-13: 978-0-7390-4713-2
Medium Low Accompaniment CD (27463)   ISBN-10: 0-7390-4717-5   ISBN-13: 978-0-7390-4717-0
Medium Low Book & CD (27464)   ISBN-10: 0-7390-4715-9   ISBN-13: 978-0-7390-4715-6

1. ANYTHING GOES

Arranged by
JAY ALTHOUSE

Words and Music by
COLE PORTER

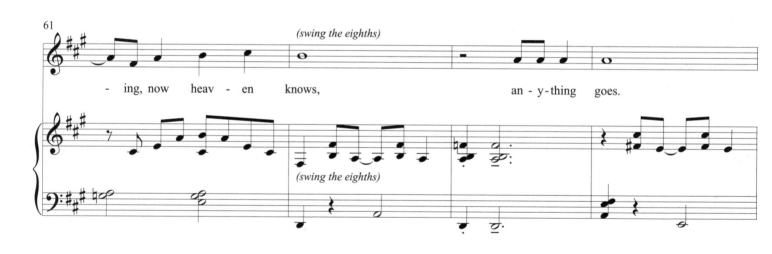

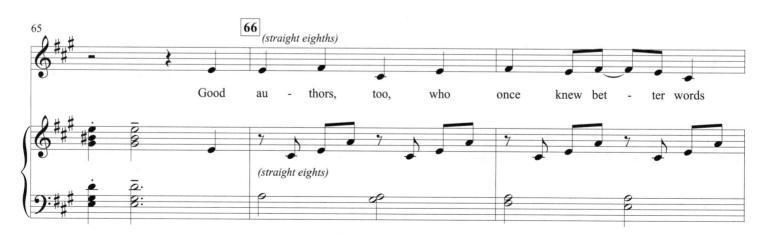

now on - ly use four let - ter words, writ - ing prose, an - y - thing goes. The world___ has gone mad to - day,___ and good's bad to - day,___ and black's white to - day,___ and day's night to - day,___ when most guys to - day___ that wo - men prize to - day___ are just

(swing the eighths)

2. AT LAST

Arranged by
JAY ALTHOUSE

Music by **HARRY WARREN**
Lyrics by **MACK GORDON**

3. BLUES IN THE NIGHT
(My Mama Done Tol' Me)

Arranged by
JAY ALTHOUSE

Words by **JOHNNY MERCER**
Music by **HAROLD ARLEN**

4. DON'T GET AROUND MUCH ANYMORE

Arranged by
JAY ALTHOUSE

Music by **DUKE ELLINGTON**
Lyrics by **BOB RUSSELL**

Missed the Sat-ur-day dance,   heard they crowd-ed the floor.

Dar - ling, I guess my mind's more at ease,___ but

nev - er - the - less, why stir up mem-o - ries?___ Been in - vit - ed on dates,

might have gone, but what for? Aw - f'lly dif - f'rent with-out

___ you,___ don't get a - round much an - y - more.

27462

5. EV'RY TIME WE SAY GOODBYE

Arranged by
JAY ALTHOUSE

Words and Music by
COLE PORTER

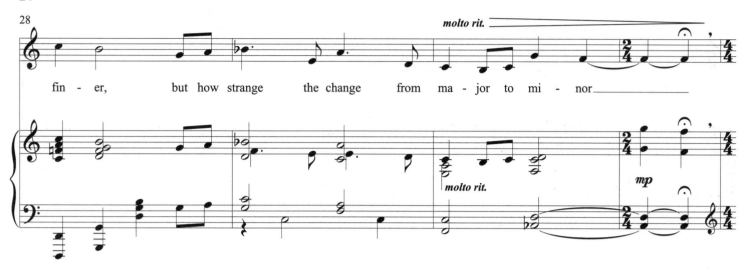

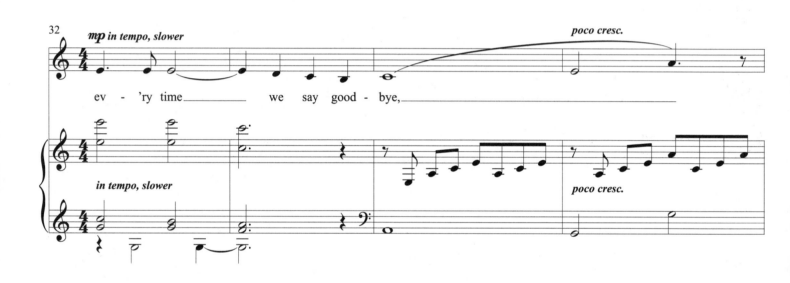

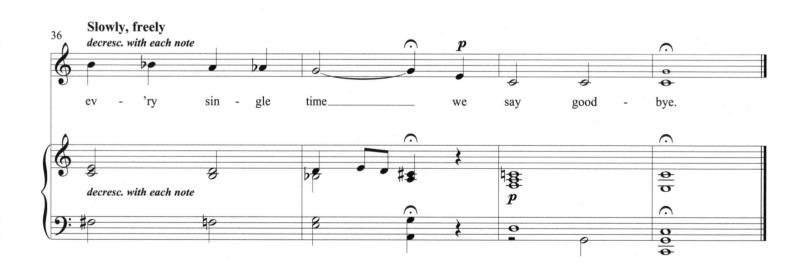

6. I ONLY HAVE EYES FOR YOU/
THE MORE I SEE YOU

Arranged by
JAY ALTHOUSE

5 *I ONLY HAVE EYES FOR YOU*
Words by Al Dubin, Music by Harry Warren

27462

7. LULLABY OF BROADWAY
(and FORTY-SECOND STREET)

Arranged by
JAY ALTHOUSE

Words by **AL DUBIN**
Music by **HARRY WARREN**

27462

27462

8. MORE THAN YOU KNOW

Arranged by
JAY ALTHOUSE

Words by **WILLIAM ROSE**
and **EDWARD ELISCU**
Music by **VINCENT YOUMANS**

27462

38

27462

9. SEND IN THE CLOWNS

Arranged by
JAY ALTHOUSE

Words and Music by
STEPHEN SONDHEIM

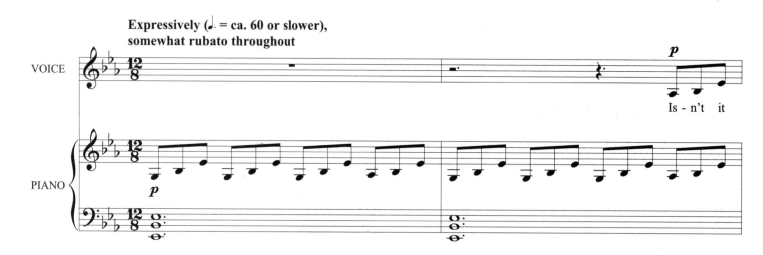

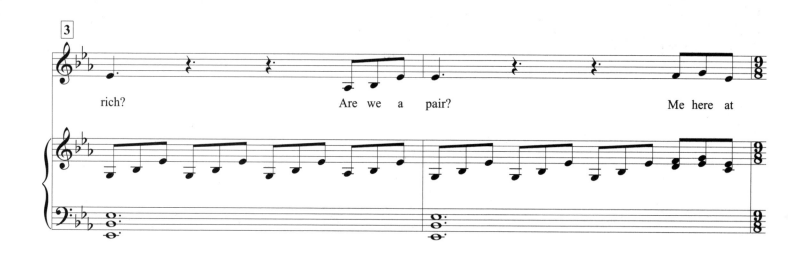

23
24
Don't you love farce?
Is - n't it rich?
My fault, I
Is - n't it
25
fear.
queer,
I thought that
los - ing my
you'd want what I want.
tim - ing this late
Sor - ry, my
in my ca -
27
dear.
reer?
But where are the clowns?
And where are the clowns?
There ought to be
Quick, send in the
29
1.
holding back
a tempo
mf
clowns.
Don't both - er, they're here.
What a sur -
holding back
a tempo
mf

Fine ‖ (*optional ending, as sung in "A Little Night Music")

* If performing this version, skip the first and second endings, and go directly from m. 28 to m. 35.

10. SKYLARK

Arranged by
JAY ALTHOUSE

Words by **JOHNNY MERCER**
Music by **HOAGY CARMICHAEL**

but my heart is___ rid-ing on your wings. So if you see them,___ an-y-

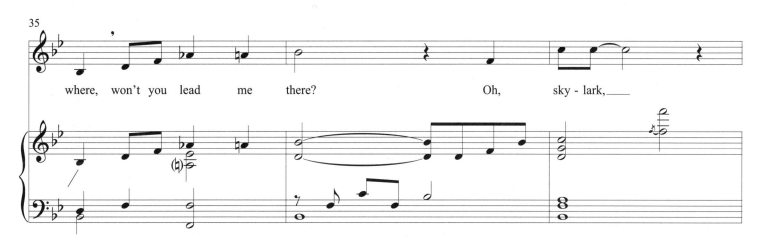

where, won't you lead me there? Oh, sky-lark,___

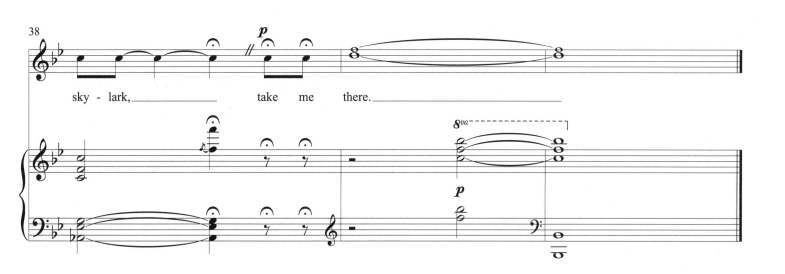

sky-lark,_____ take me there._____

11. SOMEONE TO WATCH OVER ME

Arranged by
JAY ALTHOUSE

Music and Lyrics by **GEORGE GERSHWIN®**
and **IRA GERSHWIN™**

27462

Look - ing ev - 'ry - where; have - n't found him yet. *her* He's the big af - fair I can - *She's*

not for - get. *girl* On - ly man I ev - er think of with re -

gret. I'd like to add his in - i - tial to my *her*

mon - o - gram. Tell me,

54

27462

12. TOGETHER WHEREVER WE GO

Arranged by
JAY ALTHOUSE

Lyrics by **STEPHEN SONDHEIM**
Music by **JULE STYNE**

Lyrics (voice line):
Wher- ev- er we go,_____ what- ev- er we do,_____ we're gon- na go through_____ it to- geth- er._____

A - mi - gos,_____ to - geth - er.

Through thick and through thin,_____ all

out or all in,_____ and wheth - er it's win,_____ place, or

show,_____ with you for me and me for you, we'll

The Songwriters and the Songs

Harold Arlen ("Blues in the Night")
Born 1905, Buffalo, New York. Died 1986, New York, New York.

Harold Arlen composed some of the most popular songs of the first half of the 20th century, including "Stormy Weather," "It's Only a Paper Moon," and "Let's Fall in Love," as well as the motion picture score for *The Wizard of Oz,* which included "Over the Rainbow." Arlen worked with a variety of outstanding lyricists, including Johnny Mercer, E. Y. Harburg, Ted Koehler, and Ira Gershwin. Both harmonically and melodically, Arlen's work is very rich, possibly because he was an outstanding pianist. Although he contributed the scores for several Broadway musicals, Arlen's best work and his greatest successes were in Hollywood, for the legendary M-G-M movie musicals.

In 1941, Arlen and lyricist Johnny Mercer were hired to write a song for a Judy Garland movie entitled *Hot Nocturne.* The scene called for a song to be sung by a black man in prison after he hears a distant train whistle. Mercer's line, "My mama done tol' me," was buried deep in the lyric, but Arlen loved the line, and insisted that it be moved to the opening phrase, and that it should become the song's title. Mercer agreed to move the lyric but insisted the title remain "Blues in the Night." The movie studio agreed and renamed the picture *Blues in the Night.*

Hoagy Carmichael ("Skylark")
Born 1899, Bloomington, Indiana. Died 1981, Rancho Mirage, California.

After earning a law degree from Indiana University and a brief period as a law clerk, Hoagy Carmichael set out for New York and a career in the music business. He achieved success only after moving to California, where he began writing songs and appearing as a contract actor in motion pictures. Eventually Carmichael's songwriting career eclipsed his acting career, and he went on to write such classics as "Stardust," "Georgia on My Mind," and "Up a Lazy River." His songs were "inventive, sophisticated, and jazz-oriented," according to Alec Wilder, author of *American Popular Song.* His lyricists, including Johnny Mercer, Paul Francis Webster, and Mitchell Parish, tended to set Carmichael's melodies to lyrics with nostalgic and uniquely American images of nature and the great outdoors, leading one biographer to state that if you sing Hoagy Carmichael's songs, you "don't get indoors much."

Like most lyricists, Johnny Mercer preferred to be given a complete melody to which he would set the lyrics. Hoagy Carmichael gave Mercer a meandering melody which had been planned for a musical that never materialized. The result was "Skylark." One source has Mercer claiming to have written the lyrics in less than a half hour. But in a tribute book written after Mercer's death, Johnny's widow claims he spent nearly a year on it. The truth is probably somewhere in between, as both composers and lyricists frequently portrayed their jobs as very simple, or very difficult, depending on the circumstances.

Duke Ellington ("Don't Get Around Much Anymore")
Born 1899, Washington, DC. Died 1974, New York, New York.

Although he was better known as a band leader, Duke Ellington composed well over a thousand musical works during a 60 year span of creative activity. He contributed dozens of jazz influenced songs to the popular American song repertoire, including "It Don't Mean a Thing If It Ain't Got That Swing," "Mood Indigo," and "Satin Doll." Melodically and harmonically, his songs, especially his ballads, can be complex and demanding on singers. Many of his songs began as instrumental works, to which words were added later, some by highly regarded lyricists such as Johnny Mercer and Mitchell Parish. Throughout his life, Ellington also composed orchestral and other instrumental works for the concert stage, including orchestral suites, sacred concert works, choral music, extended works for instrumentalists and dancers, and even an opera.

Like most of Ellington's songs, "Don't Get Around Much Anymore" existed first as an instrumental work. The casual, hip lyrics, omitting opening pronouns ("Missed the Saturday dance, heard they crowded the floor.") are by Bob Russell. Russell was known as a "jazz lyricist" though he continued writing lyrics for pop songs through the 1960s.

George Gershwin ("Someone to Watch Over Me")
Born 1898, Brooklyn, New York. Died 1937, Hollywood, California.

In a career that lasted less than 20 years, George Gershwin established himself as one of America's greatest songwriters and composers. He was equally at home as a writer of popular song (such as "I Got Rhythm" and "Embraceable You") and as a composer of concert works (such as *Rhapsody in Blue* and *Concerto in F*). Along with his brother Ira, a lyricist, George wrote the scores for many successful Broadway musicals, including *Of Thee I Sing,* the first musical comedy to win a Pulitzer Prize. His masterpiece, however, was the opera *Porgy and Bess,* set in South Carolina, and based on a novel by DuBose Heyward. By the mid-1930s, George had also written scores for several successful Hollywood movies and was frequently associated with the great film musicals of Fred Astaire. But he remained the quintessential New York songwriter, and was probably most comfortable writing for the Broadway stage.

Although it is almost always sung as a ballad, "Someone to Watch Over Me," was originally performed with the tempo indication *scherzando* when it was introduced in the 1926 musical *Oh! Kay!* It has been recorded by everyone from Frank Sinatra (in 1942) to Willie Nelson, though it is more frequently sung by a female. It's one of Ira Gershwin's best lyrics; note the inner rhyme in the bridge: "man some" with "handsome."

Ira Gershwin ("Someone to Watch Over Me")
Born 1896, Brooklyn, New York. Died 1983, Beverly Hills, California.

Ira Gershwin's skill as a lyricist was often overshadowed by his brother George's musical brilliance. Yet Ira was so respected and admired by other lyricists that they called him "The Jeweler" because of the precision with which he practiced his craft. On the Broadway stage, Ira was one of the first to use song lyrics to advance the plot of a show. And when work on George's opera *Porgy and Bess* bogged down with librettist DuBose Heyward, Ira was brought in to finish the project. Less well known were Ira's collaborations with songwriters other than his brother, both before his partnership with George, and after George's untimely death. Well into the 1950s, Ira continued to contribute lyrics to songs by such writers as Harold Arlen and Jerome Kern, and collaborate on theater and film works with composers such as Kurt Weill and Aaron Copland.

Johnny Mercer ("Blues in the Night" and "Skylark")
Born 1909, Savannah, Georgia. Died 1976, Bel-Air, California.

Johnny Mercer began his career as an actor who picked up a little extra money by contributing songs and lyrics to Broadway revues. Eventually he became one of America's most successful lyricists and songwriters, collaborating with many of the great writers of his era, including Harold Arlen, Harry Warren, Hoagy Carmichael, and Henry Mancini. Best known as a lyricist, he occasionally set his lyrics to his own music. His best work was done for Hollywood, and four of his songs won Academy Awards® for Best Song. Mercer was one of the founders, in 1942, of Capitol Records, had great success as a singer, and was one of the top-selling recording artists of the late 1940s. Stylistically, Mercer's lyrics had no boundaries; they could be melancholy and sad, or bright and upbeat, and often reflected his southern roots.

Cole Porter ("Anything Goes" and "Ev'ry Time We Say Goodbye")
Born 1891, Peru, Indiana. Died 1964, Santa Monica, California.

Cole Porter wrote his first songs as a student at Yale, and, after graduation, decided songwriting would be more fun than the business career his father had planned for him. Initially he had little success and moved to Paris to hone his craft, where he studied with composer Vincent d'Indy. Upon his return to the United States, Porter immediately scored successes on the Broadway stage, writing both words and music for several popular musicals. Although he also wrote for Hollywood, Porter had an almost continuous string of hits on Broadway from the 1930s through the early 1950s, including *Anything Goes* and *Kiss Me, Kate*. His songs are invariably described as "sophisticated." The form of Porter's songs are often complex. He was one of the few songwriters of his era who wrote both music and lyrics.

The musical *Anything Goes,* with book by Guy Bolton and P. G. Wodehouse, and music and lyrics by Cole Porter, opened in November, 1934 and ran for 420 performances. The title song "Anything Goes" was sung by Ethel Merman. Only the first refrain ("In olden days, a glimpse of stocking...") is printed here, though there were two other refrains which Porter revised over the years. The third line ("...now heaven knows,") was originally "But now, God knows."

"Ev'ry Time We Say Goodbye" comes from the 1944 show *Seven Lively Arts,* with book by George S. Kaufman and Ben Hecht. The show was essentially a revue, and included, among other things, a ballet with music especially composed by Igor Stravinsky. "Ev'ry Time We Say Goodbye" is one of the most passionate parting songs in the great American songbook.

Stephen Sondheim ("Send in the Clowns" and "Together Wherever We Go")
Born 1930, New York, New York.

As a young boy, Stephen Sondheim was greatly influenced by his neighbor, the lyricist and producer Oscar Hammerstein II. Sondheim began as a lyricist, collaborating with Leonard Bernstein on the songs for the groundbreaking musical *West Side Story* in 1957. In short order, he also penned the lyrics for *Gypsy,* then began writing both words and music for his shows. The first musical for which he wrote both words and music, *Company,* in 1970, began a string of hits which continues into the 21st century. Sondheim's music, as well as his lyrics, can be complex. His music has stretched tonality on the Broadway stage, and his lyrics can be both ambiguous and urbane. For the most part, Sondheim's Broadway songs have not crossed over as popular hits; they tend to be closely wedded to the context of their particular shows. Yet this is exactly what makes them successful within a show.

"Send in the Clowns" is considered by many critics to be one of the finest songs of the American musical theater. It was introduced in Sondheim's critically acclaimed 1973 show *A Little Night Music,* which won Tony Awards® for Best Musical and Best Original Score. The second verse was added for a subsequent recording by Barbra Streisand. The arrangement included here can be performed with the two verses, or as sung in *A Little Night Music,* (with a brief piano interlude) by omitting the first and second endings, and skipping from measure 28 to measure 35.

Jule Styne ("Together Wherever We Go")
Born 1905, London, England. Died 1994, New York, New York.

Jule Styne's career as a songwriter didn't take off until the 1940s when, as a band leader, he was befriended by singer Frank Sinatra, for whom he wrote a string of hits with lyricist Sammy Cahn. Styne began writing for the Broadway stage in 1947 and achieved success there with more than 20 shows over the next 30 years. His most well known shows include *Peter Pan, Gypsy,* and *Funny Girl.* Styne collaborated with a who's who of Broadway lyricists, including Betty Comden and Adolph Green, Bob Merrill, and Stephen Sondheim. His songs are in the classic Broadway style, well crafted to show off the talents of singers.

"Together Wherever We Go" comes from the Broadway musical *Gypsy,* which opened on May 21, 1959, was directed and choreographed by the legendary Jerome Robbins, and ran for 702 performances. It is a classic Broadway belter, made to order for the show's star, Ethel Merman.

Harry Warren
("At Last," "I Only Have Eyes for You/The More I See You," and "Lullaby of Broadway [and Forty-Second Street]")
Born 1893, Brooklyn, New York. Died 1981, Los Angeles, California.

Harry Warren is undoubtedly one of the most prolific of the great American songwriters. Less well known than many of his contemporaries, Warren nevertheless wrote an impressive string of hits for Hollywood from the mid 1920s through the 1940s. He collaborated with many of the great lyricists of his day, and won three Academy Awards® for Best Song. Some of his most popular works include "Chattanooga Choo Choo," "Lullaby of Broadway," and "We're in the Money." Warren's music was well suited for Hollywood: big, brassy, and full of show-biz pizzazz. He continued to write motion picture scores into the 1960s.

"At Last," (lyrics by Mack Gordon) was written for the motion picture *Sun Valley Serenade* in 1941. "I Only Have Eyes for You" (lyrics by Al Dubin) comes from the 1934 motion picture *Dames,* and "The More I See You" (lyrics by Mack Gordon) from the 1945 motion picture *Diamond Horseshoe.*

"Lullaby of Broadway" (lyrics by Al Dubin) was originally written for the motion picture *Gold Diggers of 1935,* and "Forty-Second Street" (also with lyrics by Al Dubin) for the 1933 motion picture *Forty-Second Street.* Both songs were interpolated into the 1980 Broadway musical, *42nd Street,* which ran for 3,486 performances, and was revived in 2001.

Vincent Youmans ("More Than You Know")
Born 1898, New York, New York. Died 1946, Denver, Colorado.

After serving in the armed forces in World War I, Vincent Youmans returned to New York City as a rehearsal pianist and song plugger for a music publisher. This led him to begin writing songs for musical revues. In the 1920s, he achieved some success on the Broadway stage, including the smash hit of 1925, *No, No, Nanette.* His two biggest song hits, "Tea for Two" and "I Want to Be Happy," came from that show. In addition to songwriting, he also produced a number of Broadway shows and revues. Youmans was less prolific than many of his contemporaries, and, except for a few unsuccessful shows, essentially stopped writing in the mid 1930s.

"More Than You Know" comes from one of Youmans' Broadway flops, a 1929 show entitled *Great Day.* It has a lengthy verse, which could almost stand alone. Alec Wilder, in his definitive book *American Popular Song,* considers it Youmans' finest ballad.

About the Arranger

Jay Althouse received a B.S. degree in Music Education and an M.Ed. degree in Music from Indiana University of Pennsylvania, from which he received the school's Distinguished Alumni award in 2004. For eight years he served as a rights and licenses administrator for a major educational music publisher. During that time he served a term on the Executive Board of the Music Publishers Association of America.

As a writer of choral music, Mr. Althouse has over 500 works in print for choirs of all levels. He is a writer member of ASCAP and is a regular recipient of the ASCAP Special Award for his compositions in the area of standard music. He has compiled and arranged a number of highly regarded vocal solo collections, including most of the "...for Solo Singers" series.

Mr. Althouse is a student of popular song, and believes that the songs of America's songwriters of the first half of the 20th century are as fine an example of through-composed song as can be found in western music. He believes these songs should be a part of the repertoire of all vocalists. As a composer, he has been greatly influenced by many of the songwriters and lyricists in this collection.